THE VERY BEST OF THE COMMON MAN

Rasipuram Krishnaswamy Laxman was born in Mysore in 1924. He began cartooning for the *Free Press Journal*, a newspaper in Bombay, in 1947, soon after he graduated from the University of Mysore. Six months later he joined the *Times of India* as staff cartoonist; he continued to draw for the newspaper until recently.

R.K. Laxman has written and published numerous short stories, essays and travel articles, some of which have been collected in *The Distorted Mirror*. He has also written three works of fiction, *The Hotel Riviera*, *The Messenger* and *Servants of India*, all of which have been published by Penguin Books India. Penguin has also published several collections of Laxman's cartoons in the series *The Best of Laxman* and *Laugh with Laxman*, as well as his autobiography, *The Tunnel of Time*, and most recently *Brushing Up the Years: A Cartoonist's History of India, 1947 to the Present*.

Laxman has won numerous awards for his cartoons, including Asia's top journalism award, the Ramon Magsaysay Award, in 1984. In 2005 the Government of India honoured him with the Padma Vibhushan.

He lives in Mumbai.

THE VERY BEST OF THE
COMMON MAN

PENGUIN BOOKS

An imprint of Penguin Random House

PENGUIN BOOKS

USA | Canada | UK | Ireland | Australia
New Zealand | India | South Africa | China

Penguin Books is part of the Penguin Random House group of companies
whose addresses can be found at global.penguinrandomhouse.com

Published by Penguin Random House India Pvt. Ltd
4th Floor, Capital Tower 1, MG Road,
Gurugram 122 002, Haryana, India

Penguin
Random House
India

First published by Penguin Books India 2012

10 9 8 7 6 5 4 3 2

ISBN 9780143418719

Typeset in Sabon MT by Eleven Arts, New Delhi

Printed at Repro India Limited

www.penguin.co.in

FSC
www.fsc.org

MIX
Paper from
responsible sources
FSC® C047271

INTRODUCTION

Just over a century ago the art of cartooning came to India from England and struck roots. Although other forms of art like sculpture, poetry and painting had flourished in our country for centuries, the art of graphic satire and humour was unknown. Of course both satire and humour did exist in folklore and popular poetry, poking fun at the follies of men and monarchs; the funny antics and humorous articles of the court jester were really satirical comments used to gently bring a wayward king and his band of courtiers back on track.

The role of today's cartoonist is not unlike that of the court jester of yore. His business in a democracy is to exercise his right to criticize, ridicule, find fault with and demolish the establishment and political leaders, through cartoons and caricatures.

When the British ruled, the freedom allowed to the press was limited. The role of editorial comments and cartoons was largely confined to tackling social evils like child marriage, child labour and the dowry system, or praising the efforts of the reformers. They hardly ever touched on political subjects.

Some years later the Indian cartoonist began to make timid forays into political matters. But he confined himself to attacking symbols—John Bull, for instance. When our struggle for independence from imperial domination began to gather momentum, the cartoonist gained the courage to depict real characters: the political leaders, and the viceroys and governors who were the guardians of imperial authority. Enslaved India was symbolized by an image of a suffering Indian woman called Bharat Mata—a semi-divine being adorning a crown with flowing black tresses wearing a carefully draped sari. The lady did indeed serve the purpose of inspiring patriotism in the heart of the people, inviting them to free themselves from the shackles of British imperialism.

When the British left, our leaders, who had fought for independence, settled down to draw up a respectable Constitution which would ensure freedom and equality for people who had been denied democratic liberty for centuries. India was declared a sovereign secular republic in which every citizen would enjoy liberty, equality and fraternity. The freedom of the press became particularly sacred. It was one of the most important checks to be imposed on our democratic institutions. Having drawn up such a magnificent Constitution, the leaders and the led sat themselves down and looked forward to a life of peace and prosperity.

If things had worked the way our founding fathers had hoped, the cartoonist would have become an extinct species long ago. But fortunately for the cartoonist, both the rulers and the ruled unintentionally became champions of the cartoonist's cause and ceaselessly provided grist to his mill.

When Nehru took over as prime minister, it soon became apparent to the cartoonist that he could look forward to an exciting career ahead. The aspirations of linguistic chauvinists, cow-protectors, prohibitionists, name-changers of parks and streets, all began to make their ludicrous appearance on the national scene. Our political activities became equally uproarious from the satirist's point of view. Our leaders introduced an altogether new style of functioning in our political life—hitherto unknown to the ordinary citizen. News about political parties did not concern their ideologies or their plans to help the common man, but detailed instead how intra-party groups worked against each other, squabbled amongst themselves, parted company from the party to form a new one, or defected to the very party they had opposed tooth and nail until that very moment. All this led to curiouser and curiouser political behaviour—dharnas, floor-crossing, booth-capturing, 'toppling' a chief minister, and what have you. Naturally, a cartoonist, even one with limited talent, could flourish effortlessly in this atmosphere. So, within a decade of independence, the tribe of cartoonists proliferated. New dailies, weeklies and fortnightlies published in every feasible language mushroomed everywhere, thus opening up vast opportunities for the cartoonist.

As a nation we are rather prone to talk politics—whether at a bus-stand or in a railway compartment, hobnobbing at an exclusive cocktail party or jogging in a public park. Of course, what passes for politics in these sessions is really gossip—rumour, hearsay or scandal rooted in some blurred misrepresentation of facts—concocted into a palatable mixture that is masticated between reading newspapers and magazines and listening to political news on the radio or television. That is why, though not all Indian publications are political in content, most allow for a page or two of political satire and caricature, in acknowledgement of our national pastime. Thus, the country that didn't have a single cartoonist less than a century ago is now swarming with them: good, bad and indifferent.

As I became more and more entrenched in watching and commenting on the political phantasmagoria of our country I needed an acceptable symbol to define the common Indian in my cartoons. For the cartoonist, time is of the essence and the political cartoonist has the Damocles' sword of deadlines hanging permanently over his head. Many precious minutes would be lost if I were to draw elaborate masses of people composed of Maharashtrians, Bengalis, Tamilians, Punjabis and Assamese. It is easy for the cartoonist in the West where the dress and appearance of people are largely standardized, but in India there is no way of classifying an individual by the dress he wears. An industrialist, say a textile tycoon, may be dressed exactly like a retail fruit seller. Again, a scholar of Sanskrit, English, Greek and Latin might look like the humble priest of an old impoverished temple. How was I to discover and portray the common denomination in this medley of characters, dresses, appearances and habits?

In the early days, I used to cram in as many figures as I could into a cartoon to represent the masses. Gradually I began to concentrate on fewer and fewer figures. These my readers came to accept as representative of the whole country. It would have been awfully anachronistic if I had attempted to prolong the presence of the Bharat Mata figure in my cartoons to symbolize the common people and their post-Independence turmoils. It would have been ridiculous, indeed, if Bharat Mata, with her crown and untied hair, holding our national flag, was seen hanging around in the background at a cabinet meeting, a glittering state banquet for a visiting foreign dignitary, or at the airport watching a worried minister dash off to Delhi. It would also not do to portray the common man in any manner one fancied, as many cartoonists did: sometimes as an old man in rags, sometimes as an emaciated individual and so on, bearing the legend 'The Common Man' on the hem of his clothes.

Eventually, I succeeded in reducing my symbol to one man: a man in a checked coat, whose bald head boasts only a wisp of white hair, and whose bristling moustache lends support to a bulbous nose, which in turn holds up an oversized pair of glasses. He has a permanent look of bewilderment on his face. He is ubiquitous. Today he is found hanging around a cabinet room where a high-powered meeting is in progress. Tomorrow he is among the slum dwellers listening to their woes, or marching along with protestors as they demand the abolition of the nuclear bomb. That, of course, does not preclude him from being present at a banquet hosted by the prime minister for a visiting foreign dignitary. This man has survived all sorts of domestic crises for forty years, long after the politicians who professed to protect him have disappeared. He is tough and durable. Like the mute millions of our country, he has not uttered a word in all the years he has been around. He is a silent, bewildered, and often bemused spectator of events which anyway are beyond his control.

Besides my usual 'big' cartoons, I started a series called *You Said It*. A single column cartoon appeared every day in the *Times of India*, in the right hand corner of the front page. The idea was to make it a free-wheeling comment on socio-economic and sociopolitical aspects, free of real political personalities or actual political events. The feature did not attempt any serious analysis but reflected, with a certain conscious irreverence, the general mood of the country as a

whole. I expected this column to appeal to readers who were
not too critical and who accepted their humdrum lot without
a murmur. My taciturn Common Man, who was appearing off
and on in my bigger cartoons in the company of Nehru and his
cabinet ministers, came in handy for this purpose. The other
characters I built around him in this single column cartoon
were villagers, bureaucrats, ministers, crooked businessmen,
economic experts, rebellious students, factory workers—in
fact nearly every type, from every walk of life, as the occasion
warranted. The column proved to be extremly popular. It has
appeared every day for more than half a century, except on
those all-too-brief occasions when I am on holiday!

Gathered in this volume is a selection from the cartoons I
have done over the last few years. I am continually surprised
to note that most of them are timeless in their relevance to
any given moment in our history.

R.K. Laxman

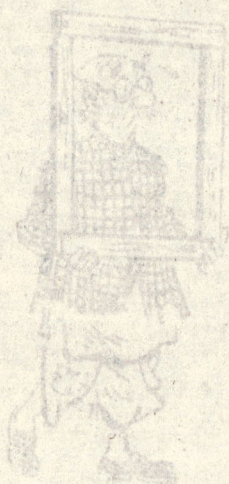

The history of election campaigning in India.

Of course, we have progressed a great deal. First they were coming by bullock-cart, then by jeep and now this!

A marvellously illustrated cartoon of the filth a politician must stride through to rise to power.

No, *they don't mind wading through it. After all, it comes only once in five years, during the elections.*

A fundamental bafflement.

I can't understand these people. Not a soul here knows how to read or write and yet they want a school.

Never mind that none of last election's promises
were kept. Note the caricature of the politician's
right-hand man, in shades.

*Last elections, if you remember, I promised water supply,
drainage and clean living conditions. This time I promise . . .*

Some wishes are easier to grant than others!

I was afraid they would demand drinking water, schools, etc.
Luckily they only want a separate state.

People's demands are rising.

A drinking water tap here and a school there won't do! For him to win this constituency, you have to give these people an aerodrome, a TV station, an atomic reactor complex!

A promise fulfilled.

I think he has been elected. You asked him for drinking water
when he came on his election tour, remember?

Five years later . . .

*No, sir, it was not there when you visited your constituency last.
It was just a sapling you planted then!*

The visiting politician is identified more by his
vehicle than by his deeds.

There he is! He comes regularly every year to lay the foundation stones for new projects: hydroelectric, housing, industrial complex, etc. . . .!

A politician's accomplishments will never go uncelebrated in India.

—wiped out corruption, improved the lot of the common man,
brought prosperity and plenty, when he governed as the chief
minister between 17th March 1967 AD and 24th March 1967 AD.

Some things never change.

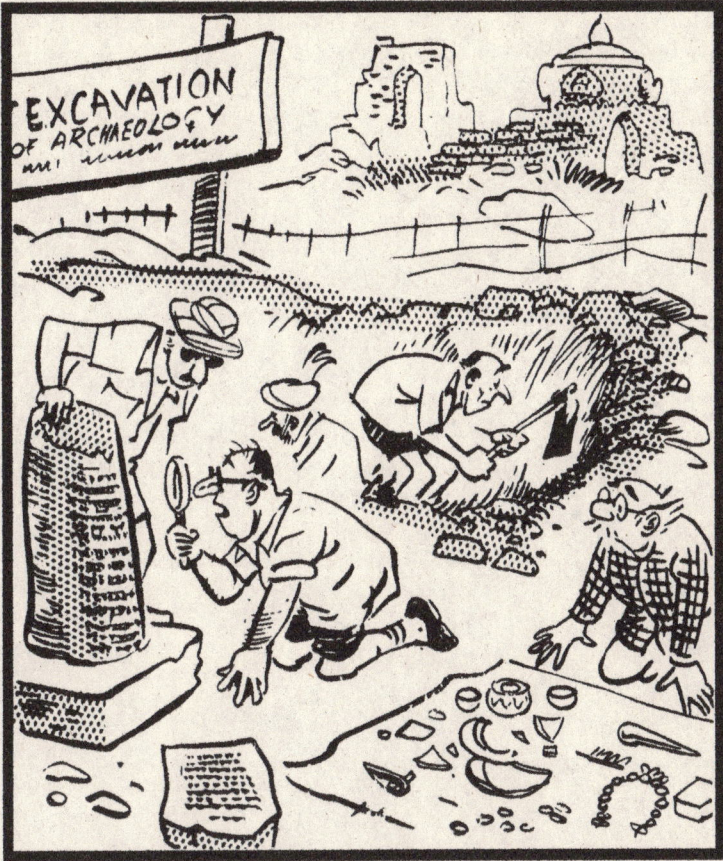

. . . and the ruler goes on to assure his subjects that he will eradicate poverty, unemployment . . .

This is one of Laxman's favourite jokes—a visiting politician made to wear a dunce cap in the name of traditional headgear in a remote outpost.

They are fooling him. There is no such traditional headgear in this region!

As Laxman shows us again and again, one of the
funniest things about politicians is that they don't
seem to realize what they are saying.

Like in all previous elections, I have come once more to seek your valuable vote so that I can win and continue to improve your living conditions . . .

A hilarious take on anti-terrorism rhetoric that politicians resort to, again without thinking.

These blasts were masterminded to deal a body-blow to our economy, cripple our progress and reduce us to poverty . . .

One of the problems with larger-than-life
political figures.

If the prices have shot up, couldn't you have ordered a small cut-out? This has used up all the campaign funds!

At their most memorable, Laxman's characters are very literal. Rushing to the well of the house to protest is of course a rather quintessentially Indian parliamentary phenomenon.

He came and immediately rushed to the well of that house!
Must be an Opposition MP!

What, after all, are politicians for?

We saw the TV, saw you walk-out, rush to the well, create pandemonium! We are grateful, you do so much to improve our life, sir.

The effects of Parliament are far-reaching.

*Hear the din, the noise, the uproar? That means the
House is in session!*

The travails of coalition politics.

Forty-seven will support? That's great! . . . What, thirty-one,
is it? . . . That's OK. It's only fourteen? Actually nine . . .
the final figure is three . . .?

Outside support—another key element
of coalition politics.

No, sir, we can't draw the curtains. They are there to support
you from the outside, as promised!

At least in their names, political parties do
try to be all-inclusive.

Don't announce yet! He threatens to quit if the words 'Front', 'March' and 'Kisan' are not included in the name of our new party!

If you have ever wondered why politicians are so interested in Kashmir . . .

*Can I at least go this country to find a peaceful solution to
the Kashmir problem, please? I have not been abroad
even once, you see!*

A remarkable office, with a driveway right behind the desk, to make going off on foreign trips easier.

By the way, tell me what bilateral talks I should have on what,
with whom?

An Indian minister abroad.

*Ah! What's that? A factory? Manufactures what? . . . Do come
over to our country to start one like that!*

It is easy enough to confuse one minister with another, especially if you're looking at effigies.

You fool! I ordered the effigy of the minister for agriculture.
This one is of the minister for housing!

Laxman's visual humour at its best.

That's a part of the anti-corruption drive, I am told, sir.

Visual and literal humour combine superbly in
this cartoon.

Ah, removed it! But this happening once too often. I would advise you to resign from politics.

One of Laxman's excellent cartoons which eloquently tells the story of an incident that has happened a few minutes ago.

*It went off very well, thank you, except that he didn't see the
flower pot near his feet . . .*

One for the camera.

It is for showing at the election meetings how clean he is.

The problem with percentages is that sometimes they
don't add up to a round 100!

There seems to be something wrong in your calculation,
sir! Backward Class 55%, ST 30%, KP 21%, PC, NC and
so on add up to 273%!

At the core of every good speech is data that speaks for itself.

I have worked out some interesting figures—12.8%, 14.7%,
1.5% only, 22.3%! Incorporate these in my speech.

Who says the government doesn't have a grip
on inflation?

Who says the government doesn't have a grip
on inflation?

Not to worry, sir! It's under strict control. We held it at 9.10%.
Then again at 9.75%. Later we put the breaks at 10.70%.
Now we will arrest it at 11.75% . . .

At the planning stage, scenarios do tend to look very much rosier than reality.

Further up. Up, a little to the right and up—that's it! And now let us set about achieving it!

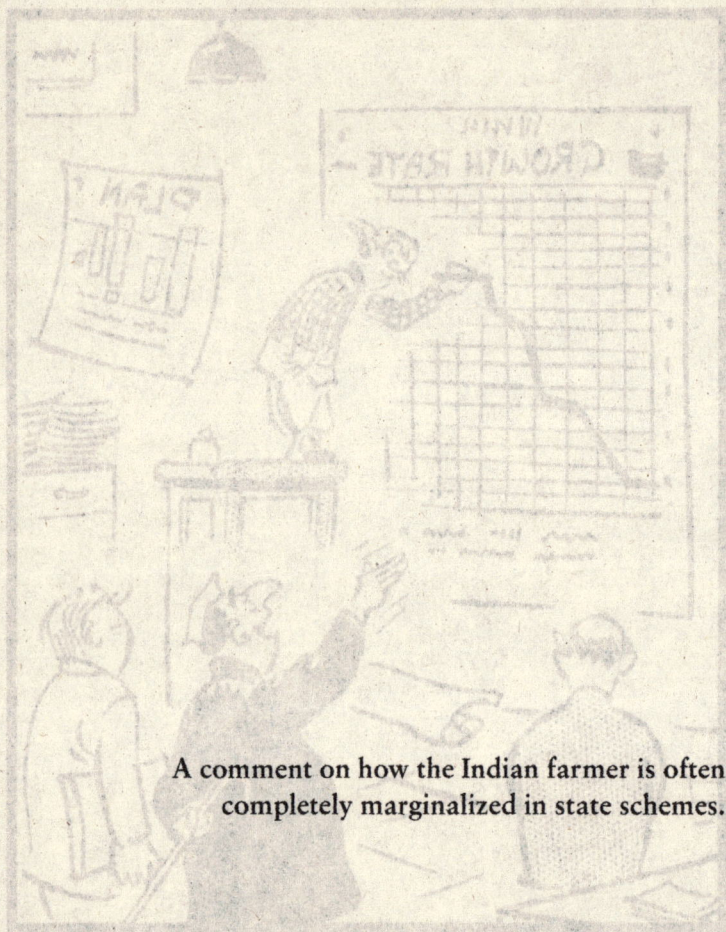

A comment on how the Indian farmer is often completely marginalized in state schemes.

We are all here, sir—fertilizer supplier, pest controller, seed adviser and soil tester—but I wonder who that man is standing over there!

Apart from the quality of Laxman's artistry that conjures up devastation with a few simple brushstrokes, this cartoon is memorable also for its telling comment that we come to find out what our resources and habitats are worth only through calamity.

Sixty thousand crores loss! But for the cyclone we would never have known we were so rich!

The priority in a flood-hit area, of course, is to greet
the VIP who would soon arrive for a flying visit.

*My dear chap, some VIP is bound to visit this place! The flood
has created havoc here, you see!*

It is sometimes difficult to tell the difference between man-made and natural destruction.

*Tell me, am I touring the cyclone-ravaged area or the
riot-affected area?*

And sometimes it's difficult to tell the difference between what's been damaged and what hasn't.

The blast damage is over here, sir!

Rural development.

80

*Oh yes, this village has improved a lot, sir—it's almost like a
big city now—no water, no electricity here either!*

Development is the bane of the poor . . .

If this project comes up here we will be finished!

It's not just ancient ruins that are in a shambles.

No, not this, sir. This is his home. The ancient ruin, for the restoration of which a hundred crore rupees has been sanctioned, is over there!

The markers of progress are sometimes mere status symbols.

No trains, just a station to make the place look a little
progressive. The new minister is from here, you see!

A national downturn is felt most keenly on the streets.

Things have gone from bad to worse. This used to be such a posh pavement when I moved in here!

What does economic growth really mean to the common man? How does it shape their ambitions?

*If the economic prospects really brighten I'll emigrate to the city
and look for a place on the pavement of a posh locality!*

The thing about purchasing power is that sometimes it can be more of a curse than a blessing.

Consider yourself lucky. You don't have the purchasing power
we have.

When the economy looks up, it means the nation is
on the move!

It seems the nation's economy has improved! Come, let us go on our round of begging!

Certain workers may not always succeed. Thus, the poor man, who himself has done nothing and yet might be a citizen of India.

Census workers may not always appreciate this, but a poor Indian does know that he/she could only be a citizen of India.

What, are we citizens of India? Of course, we are! Don't we look it?

Those condemned to live in unhygienic conditions are not necessarily unmindful of hygiene. To read further into this cartoon, note that the boy is reaching out towards a box of Kellogg's. The crow, Laxman's favourite creature, makes an appearance here.

*Be careful about what you eat! There are quite a few cases of
food poisoning around, I understand!*

The incongruity of a protest fast in a nation populated by starving millions is never lost on Laxman.

No, I'm not fasting, I'm starving. He is fasting.

One of the possible reasons why India doesn't
exactly thrive on foreign trade.

Nobody knows what these are! The agreement with the foreign country is that we export what it wants; and in return it gives us what we don't have. We certainly don't have these!

A cartoonist's solution to the economic downturn.

Sensex, BSE, NSE, etc. Depressing! These days I feel like watching the TV after turning it upside down!

Potholes—and the quirky repairs carried out on them—are a recurring concern for Laxman, as for most city-based Indians.

Not that, my dear man. This one. We haven't got orders to repair that.

A superbly illustrated cartoon that shows up the folly
of marketing new models of cars in a country which
doesn't have the roads where one can drive them.

'. . . *immediate delivery, easy instalments, no down payment.'
What's the use! If they offered roads too then it would be
worth having it!*

As potholes get larger and cars get smaller, this is
bound to happen at some point.

Look at that poor chap! Why can't they stop producing small
cars till these potholes are filled?

An acerbic comment on the country's education system.

No, I couldn't get admission. I got only 82% in maths, 83% in
science, 91% in social science, 89% in . . .

Another telling comment on where a university
degree will get one in India.

It is sad to see these youngsters hanging around like this for admission. Remember in our days we just walked in and got our seats?

Taxpaying citizens have a lot to worry about.

That's mine, too! But I don't live there because I don't want to give the impression of living beyond my own sources of income!

A picture speaks more than a hundred words.

—and in this I have tried to convey all my inner tension, struggle and torment!

For those who felt that hosting a beauty contest in
India would be a derogatory gesture towards
Indian womanhood.

I am proud of the spectacular transformations and improvements which are taking place among the women of India.

Not to forget the girl child.

Learn to balance it properly, silly girl! Remember, soon you will have to start working!

As many city-dwellers will attest, it does take
only a small cloud.

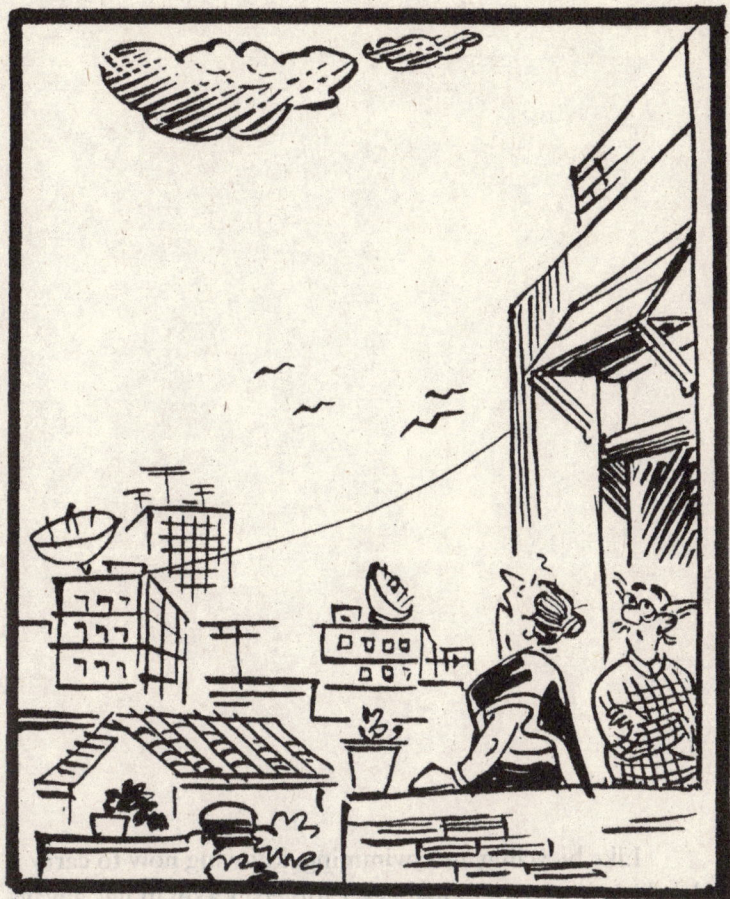

*Here it comes! There go train service, telephones,
power supply . . .*

Like bicycling and swimming, knowing how to carry a load is a lesson an Indian never forgets! Laxman has always been concerned about how heavy a child's schoolbag is, and the trauma this is bound to cause a child.

*Of course, I too went to school. Where do you think I learnt
to carry it like this?*

Children these days are way too knowledgeable.

*I don't know if the king disclosed his wealth, I don't know if his
land came under the ceiling, I don't know of the price asked for
dowry—stop asking questions and listen!*

Out-of-the-box thinking is so seldom appreciated
in a child.

What? Like Picasso? No, you must learn to draw properly and become an artist!

Who decides what's objectionable? (Tikku, by the way, is Laxman's favourite hoarding sign.)

Well, what do you say, do you think it's objectionable?
Shall we start a riot?

Endorsements are what many a celebrity is known by.

Yes, father, I know this uncle, he likes the best soft drink,
the best toothpaste, the best washing soap, the best . . .

If you're playing for India you're not just battling an opposition but also trying to combat a slew of internal problems.

*We have not done too badly, considering that we are facing an
enormous financial crisis, law and order problems besides
having a minority government at the Centre . . .*

Consumerist campaigns can go haywire sometimes.

Go at once, change the hoarding all over the country.
Our Diwali offer is just the other way round.

Crunchy Munchy Biscuits of Italy (!) and Sipco Soft Drinks of USA are two of Laxman's favourite corporate sponsors.

. . . and this speech was sponsored by Crunchy Munchy Biscuits of Italy and Sipco Soft Drinks of USA.

Another wonderful example of a cartoon that tells
the story of what has happened earlier.

You shouldn't have tried to put sweets into his mouth when you got the ticket! He hates you! I told you.

An instance of ingenious visual humour—one of the main problems of negotiating with sadhus is that you can't tell them apart!

*This morning one of you had a long discussion with me about
the present problems. May I know who it was?*

It is easy enough to confuse religious agendas with development programmes.

*When he was talking of building, construction, plans and so on,
I thought it was some housing project. And I didn't realize it
was all about a mandir.*

Apart from kickback scandals, uninformed weapon
purchases can have other drawbacks too.

*This is what will happen if we send all sorts of people to
all sorts of countries for defence purchases!*

All in a day's work.

*Don't forget—you have to renew your club membership,
your credit card, your bail period, your . . .*

It's all about how you read the message.

*We hear his call to quit India even today. My own two sons are
NRIs in the USA . . .*

Incorrect grammar must be corrected at all costs.

Sorry for interrupting you when you are talking, sir. It is not '. . . I told to you last time . . .', it is 'I told you last time . . .'

The Indian is nothing if not keenly interested in global politics.

. . . and if Mr Bush persists in his intention to attack Iraq,
we will be left with no choice but to declare a one-day
statewide total bandh!

One method. Many uses.

Quiet, please! Not 'Clinton, go back!' He's gone. Now shout,
'Roll-back LPG price hike!'

Bureaucrats are feared—for many reasons.

*I have given him over a dozen extensions so far because he says
he will write his memoirs when he retires.*

A truly absurd situation. Note the suspicious looks the security guards are giving everyone.

My purse is pickpocketed!

Another exquisite example of visual humour.

What do you expect if the delays get increasingly long?

A completely hilarious—but not entirely unlikely—scenario.

*I think we would do well to cut out this idea of welcoming the
visitors in our cultural costumes!*

Politics and Bollywood rule the nation—and sometimes they look remarkably similar.

I don't know what it is. If I could read I would have been able to tell you whether it is an election poster or a cinema poster!

The stars leave their mark on the cityscape.

It must have been a movie star going home after dinner.

Bollywood can really impact people's lives.

... you don't like me any more! Just because the studio is
on strike you don't chase me around the trees singing and
dancing like before!

The effects of Bollywood are everywhere.

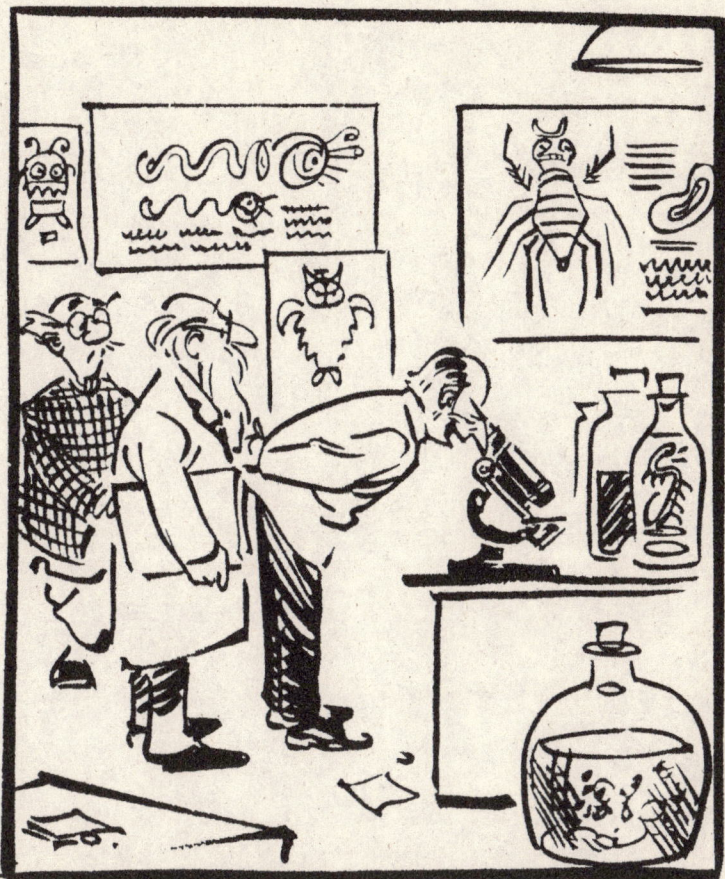

It's like in our movies—sex and violence!

One is not sure which is more irritating—the number of artificial satellites in the sky, or their robotic names.

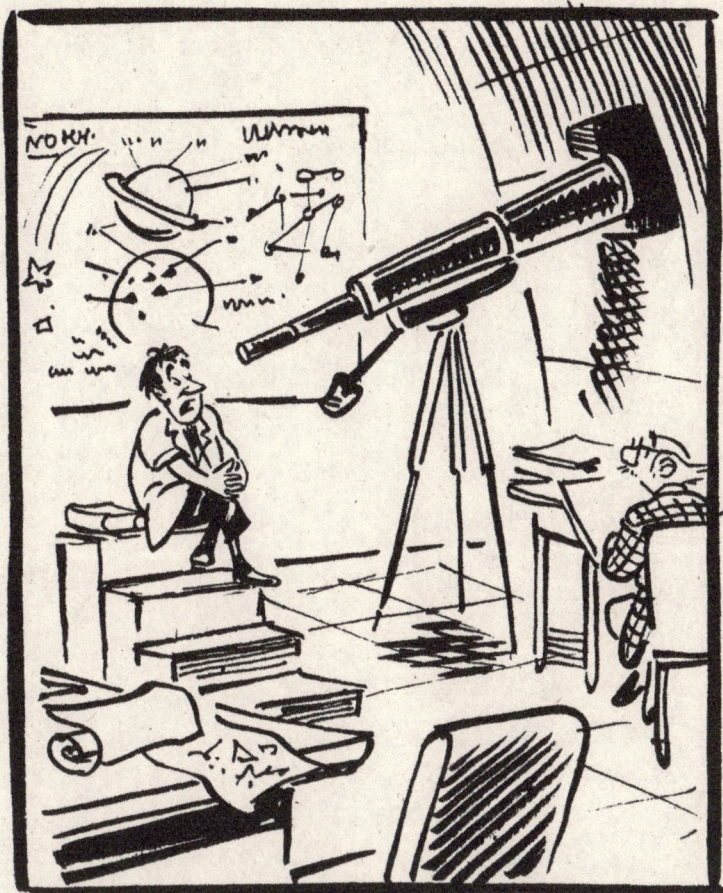

Astronomy has no future. There won't be any more studying Mars or Jupiter. It will all be INSAT-2C, 6B, . . . 10Q, . . . 27R, . . . 53Z . . . crowding the sky!

Another instance of eloquent visual humour.

In spite of all our efforts there's still a large stock of unsold cloth with us!

Drawn years ago, this cartoon foretells the most
common question asked by mediapersons today:
'How do you feel?'

I am from Media Worldwide, sir. What is your reaction to rash and careless driving?

Where flight delays on the national airlines are concerned, an astrologer's guess is as good as any!

He says, since no one in the corporation has the information,
he has come to help the passengers!

One from the olden days, when your telephone would work only once in a blue moon.

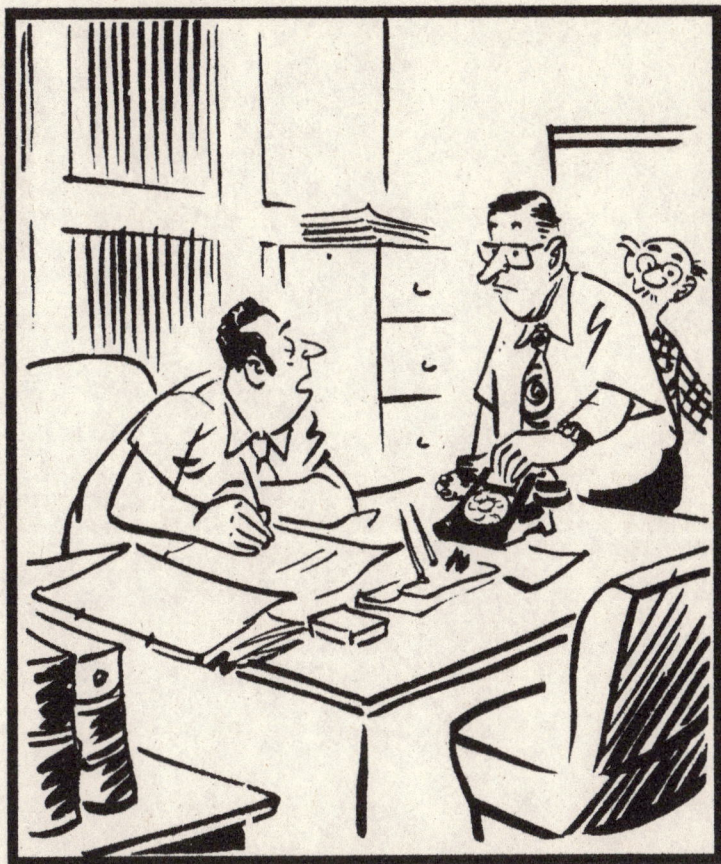

Yes, of course it works. It worked on May 4th, June 21st,
and again on the second of this month.

No one takes on the local media for accurate information

No one relies on the local media for accurate information.

Do you hear the noise coming from there? Get me the BBC.
I want to know what's going on!

The systemization of corruption.

The reputation of this office is getting from bad to worse.
That chap wants to know where to give the bribe!

There is a hierarchy among street dwellers as well.

It's my dwelling. He's my paying guest.

The Common Man's wife is a key figure in Laxman's cartoons, though she doesn't appear very regularly.

*Why so much fuss about it now? Don't we all vote with no
confidence anyway every time we vote?*

**A good instance of Laxman's ear for the tricks
language can play.**

*Anything can happen these days! Look at this legal loophole,
for instance. I bought this flat because I was assured it had a
clear sea view!*

A forever rising Sensex does cause a few problems.

I don't think it will go up any further. You can tell him to stop.

Precautionary measures.

*We got it made that way to prevent anti-social elements doing
it every now and then.*

It's not always entirely safe to fire a warning shot
in the air . . .

Sorry, sir! I fired in the air to disperse the violent mob gathered over there!

Indian geography.

Station? Go straight down Rajiv Marg, turn at Indira Circle
towards Nehru Square and then past Rajiv . . .